WORKING THE CASE

LAW ENFORCEMENT, POLICE WORK, AND POLICE ORGANIZATIONS

Law Enforcement and Intelligence Gathering

WORKING THE CASE

LAW ENFORCEMENT, POLICE WORK, AND POLICE ORGANIZATIONS

Edited by LEON MURLEY

Britannica® Educational Publishing

in association with

ROSEN
EDUCATIONAL SERVICES

Published in 2017 by Britannica Educational Publishing (a trademark of Encyclopædia Britannica, Inc.) in association with The Rosen Publishing Group, Inc.
29 East 21st Street, New York, NY 10010

Distributed exclusively by Rosen Publishing.
To see additional Britannica Educational Publishing titles, go to rosenpublishing.com.

First Edition

Britannica Educational Publishing
J.E. Luebering: Executive Director, Core Editorial
Anthony L. Green: Editor, Compton's by Britannica

Rosen Publishing
Kathy Kuhtz Campbell: Senior Editor
Nelson Sá: Art Director
Brian Garvey: Designer
Cindy Reiman: Photography Manager
Bruce Donnola: Photo Researcher
Introduction and Conclusion by Daniel E. Harmon

Library of Congress Cataloging-in-Publication Data

Names: Murley, Leon, editor.
Title: Working the case : law enforcement, police work, and police organizations / editor, Leon Murley.
Description: First edition. | New York, NY : Britannica Educational Publishing in association with The Rosen Publishing Group, Inc., 2017. | Series: Law Enforcement and Intelligence Gathering | Includes bibliographical references and index.
Identifiers: LCCN 2016020468 | ISBN 9781508103806 (library bound)
Subjects: LCSH: Police—Juvenile literature. | Law enforcement—Juvenile literature. | Crime prevention—Juvenile literature. | Criminal investigation—Juvenile literature.
Classification: LCC HV7922 .W67 2017 | DDC 363.2—dc23
LC record available at https://lccn.loc.gov/2016020468

Manufactured in China

Photo credits: Cover, p. 3 Ron Koeberer/Aurora/Getty Images; pp. 8-9 (background), 12, 24, 41, 63 hunthomas/Shutterstock.com; p. 9 The Boston Globe/Getty Images; p. 13 Odd Andersen/AFP/Getty Images; pp. 14-15 Larry W. Smith/Getty Images; pp. 18-19, 52-53 Pacific Press/LightRocket/Getty Images; pp. 22, 34, 36-37, 44, 76-77 © AP Images p. 25 Marcos Townsend/AFP/Getty Images; pp. 26-27 Rene Johnston/Toronto Star/Getty Images; p. 29 Johan Nilsson/TT/AFP/Getty Images; pp. 32-33 John Thys/AFP/Getty Images; p. 39 Thomas Imo/Photothek/Getty Images; pp. 42-43 © Peter Casolino/Alamy Stock Photo; p. 46 MPI/Archive Photos/Getty Images; pp. 48-49 Scott Olson/Getty Images News/Getty Images; p. 55 Paul J. Richards/AFP/Getty Images; pp. 56-57 Johannes Simon/Getty Images; p. 59 Kevork Djansezian/Getty Images; p. 65 Jean-Philippe Ksiazek/AFP/Getty Images; p. 67 Hrvoje Polan/AFP/Getty Images; pp. 68-69 © RosaIreneBetancourt 8/Alamy Stock Photo; p. 71 Mark Makela/Getty Images; p. 73 George W. Bush Library/NARA; pp. 78-79 George Frey/Getty Images; back cover, interior pages (background) stefano carniccio/Shutterstock.com

CONTENTS

INTRODUCTION

Police are officers who represent the civil authority of government. They are typically responsible for maintaining public order and safety, enforcing the law, and preventing, detecting, and investigating criminal activities. Police may also perform various licensing and regulatory activities.

Some police work in small towns or sparsely populated rural counties or districts. Others work in cities of many thousand or even several million citizens. Specialized police focus on tasks such as highway traffic safety, the regulation of natural resources and wildlife, and drug and alcohol law enforcement. Within the military, police forces are trained to patrol bases and enforce laws and policies on land and vessels at sea. Outside of government, officers from private security agencies patrol and guard office and industrial complexes, banks, and other institutions.

State and national governments maintain police agencies to resolve issues relevant to those larger jurisdictions. Worldwide, nations coordinate certain of their police assets to cope with terrorism and other international problems.

There is a consensus among researchers, based on a definition first proposed by American sociologist Egon Bittner, that the common feature among all the different agencies engaged in policing is their legal competence to enforce coercive, nonnegotiable measures to resolve problematic situations. Such situations are

Police officers with guns drawn react to the explosion of two bombs during an attack at the Boston Marathon on April 15, 2013. The police are often put into situations that are chaotic and dangerous.

characterized by two features: their potential for harm and the need to solve them urgently before that potential is realized.

James J. Willis, a professor in the Department of Criminology, Law and Society at George Mason University, has emphasized that law enforcement is but one task of the police. He has also observed that the organization of police entities is not the same in all countries. In the United States, he explains, police responsibilities are divided among local, state, and federal bodies. According to the US Bureau of Justice Statistics, there are more than 12,000 local police departments in the United States. Some of them employ as few as one or two officers. Others employ hundreds or thousands. In certain other countries, police operations are centralized under national umbrella organizations, with different divisions serving at local levels.

Most of the work of police officers is nonconfrontational. The variety of situations in which police are involved is much greater than law enforcement and order maintenance. For example, they provide directions and aid to citizens and assist emergency responders who work for fire and rescue services. Investigative officers spend much of their time questioning witnesses and examining digital and paper data.

This volume examines the role of police at various levels of society, from small communities to state and national jurisdictions. It addresses the concept of due process and the relationship between police and court systems, an arrangement that imposes accountability on police officers. The book considers controversial issues, such as police activities involving minorities and responses to protests and riots. It concludes with discussions of "high policing"—the involvement of police in national security—and of international police organizations such as Interpol.

Chapter One

POLICE AND SOCIETY

There is a remarkable historical, geographic, and organizational diversity in the activities of people who are, or have been, defined as police. Police work has developed considerably from what it was centuries ago. As populations grew and informal institutions of socialization and social control—such as the family, schools, and the church—decreased in effectiveness, police became increasingly necessary. However, no uniform worldwide system of policing ever emerged.

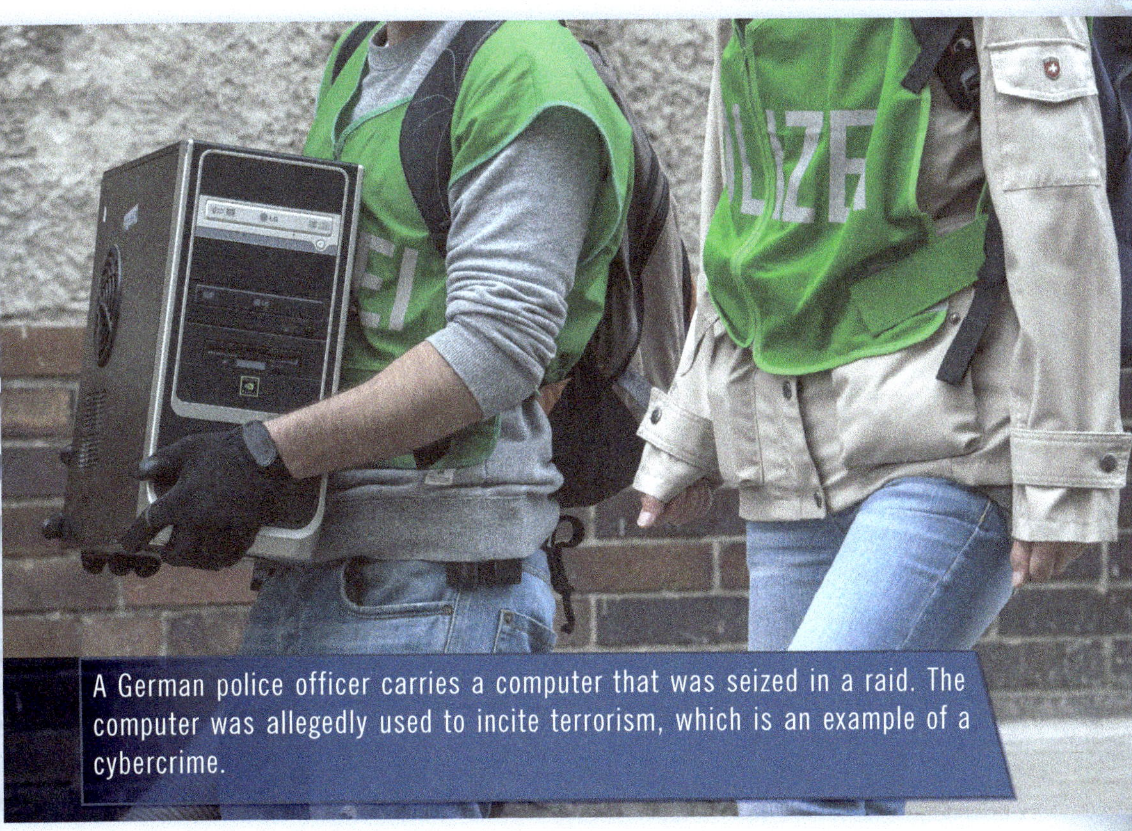

A German police officer carries a computer that was seized in a raid. The computer was allegedly used to incite terrorism, which is an example of a cybercrime.

Numerous factors help to explain the diversity of police activities and systems. The types of crime typically committed in a society and the methods used by criminals play a great part in determining a police force's activities. For instance, if criminals use firearms, the police are likely to be armed, or if criminals use computers to commit crimes, the police may establish a special unit dedicated to investigating cybercrimes. History also helps to explain this diversity; for example, former colonies tend to keep the policing system established by their colonizers. Population plays an

A deputy sheriff in Kansas scours an area where illegal drugs were produced. Law-enforcement officers in rural communities often have to patrol extensive areas and are involved in a broad range of criminal investigations.

important role as well; policing rural areas and villages vastly differs from policing large cities. Foremost

among the factors that determine a country's system of policing, however, are the political culture of the society—for example, whether it is open and democratic or closed and totalitarian—and the state's conception of police accountability.

POLICING SMALL COMMUNITIES

Most people willingly obey most laws, whether a police officer is present or not. They comply with the laws because they consider them fair and because they believe that in the long run it is in their interest to observe them. In small communities in which most citizens know each other, people who live up to the community's shared ideals are rewarded with the esteem of their fellow citizens. If they break the law or fall short of other people's expectations, their lives often become more difficult because they are shamed or shunned by the rest of the community and are less likely to receive assistance in times of trouble. In all societies, this system of informal rewards and punishments is the most potent aid to law enforcement, but it is strongest in small communities. The forces that order life in a small community thus make the task of the police much easier. Police action is needed only when such informal controls have proved insufficient.

This is why rural and sparsely populated areas are often policed by a single centralized—and often militarized—police force, even in countries that have a decentralized police system. A single police organization operating under a unified command is more cost-effective and more operationally efficient than a large number of independent small-town police forces. Since the territory to cover may be very large and characterized by difficult terrain, police in such regions must have the long-range mobility and adaptability that are characteristic of military forces. In addition, the countryside has historically been policed by military organizations, as police forces were initially created in urban settings. (The great exceptions to this model are the United Kingdom and the United States, which have long resisted police centralization.)

POLICING LARGE SOCIETIES

In larger and more complex societies, informal institutions of social control are generally weaker, and, as a result, formal institutions are generally stronger. The relative weakness of informal controls is attributable to a number of factors. In large societies people often deal with strangers whom they will never meet again, and in such circumstances there may be fewer informal rewards for honesty or fewer informal penalties for dishonesty. Such communities tend also to be more technologically advanced, which leads to the adoption of new laws, such as those regulating the licensing and operation of automobiles and those concerned with commerce conducted on the internet.

Because some of these new laws may not have the same moral significance as older laws criminalizing violence, theft, or fraud, people may feel less of an obligation to obey them. Moreover, when new laws are created, crime increases almost necessarily. There is thus a danger that people who are convicted of having violated a new law may feel aggrieved and in the future be less willing to cooperate with the police or to obey the law when they are not being observed.

Finally, as societies grow, it becomes more difficult for people to place the public interest ahead of their private interests in circumstances where the two may conflict. An employer who catches an employee committing an offense within the workplace, for example, may choose not to notify the police because he fears that the firm's production, profit, or prestige would suffer if the offense was publicly exposed.

Counterterrorism officers from the New York City Police Department screen people before the annual New Year's Eve celebration in Times Square.

POLICE AND THE STATE

A country's political culture helps to determine whether its police forces are organized nationally or locally. The desire for efficiency lends itself to the establishment of

centralized police forces, which can take advantage of coordination and savings in training, organization, and service delivery. However, such forces face the problem aptly summarized by the Latin question *Quis custodiet ipsos custodes?* ("Who guards the guardians?").

In some democratic countries, particularly the United States and, to a lesser extent, Great Britain, citizens have traditionally believed that the existence of a national police force would concentrate too much power in the hands of its directors. They have believed that local communities could not hold a national police force accountable for abuses of power, and they have feared that the national government could use such a police force to keep itself in power illegitimately. For those and other reasons, some democratic countries favor organizing police forces on a local basis. Decentralization brings the police closer to the community, and it often succeeds in tailoring policing to the specific needs of a community. However, a decentralized police apparatus tends to hinder the flow of intelligence between the various components of the system. Another drawback of a system of accountability to local government is that the narrow

DUE PROCESS

The concept of due process requires that legal proceedings are carried out only according to rules and principles that have been established to protect the rights of individuals. Mainly associated with one of the fundamental guarantees of the United States Constitution, due process originated in early English common law and constitutional history. The first concrete expression of the due process idea embraced by Anglo-American law appeared in the 39th article of the Magna Carta (1215) in the royal promise that "No freeman shall be taken or (and) imprisoned or disseised [dispossessed of land or other property] or exiled or in any way destroyed...except by the legal judgment of his peers or (and) by the law of the land." Later English laws upheld the concept of due process.

Drafters of the US Constitution adopted due process in the Fifth Amendment, ratified in 1791, which provides that "No person shall...be deprived of life, liberty, or property, without due process of law." This amendment, however, was held inapplicable to state actions that might violate an individual's constitutional rights. It was not until the ratification of the Fourteenth Amendment in 1868 that the states became subject to a federally enforceable due process restraint on their activities.

The meaning of due process has evolved over decades of controversial interpretation by the Supreme Court. Some justices have adhered to the idea that the framers of the

Fourteenth Amendment intended the entire Bill of Rights—the first ten amendments to the Constitution—to be binding on the states. They have asserted that this position would provide an objective basis for reviewing state activities and would promote uniformity between state and federal rights and sanctions. Other justices, however, have contended that states should be allowed considerable freedom in conducting their affairs, so long as they comply with a fundamental fairness standard. Ultimately, the latter position substantially prevailed, and due process was recognized as embracing only those principles of justice that are "so rooted in the traditions and conscience of our people as to be ranked as fundamental." In fact, however, almost all of the Bill of Rights has by now been included among those fundamental principles.

relationship between the police and their political overseers may encourage the corruption of both parties.

The need for police accountability is made evident by the great power that police forces wield over the lives, liberties, safety, and rights of citizens. Governments empower police to compel individuals to comply with the law; they allow officers to stop, search, detain, cite, and arrest citizens and to use physical and sometimes deadly force. If police use those powers improperly, they can abuse the civil rights of the very

Police officers in Colorado execute a search warrant at the home of an alleged criminal. Search warrants empower the police to search a place and seize property to obtain evidence in criminal investigations.

citizens they are supposed to protect. Thus, it is critical that police be accountable for their policies and behavior. In democratic countries, accountability is ensured mainly by three means. First, police forces are made subordinate to elected representatives (as in the United States, where mayors or state governors oversee the police) or to an elected police authority (as in England, Wales, and Australia). Second, the courts are entrusted to safeguard the respect of due process by the police. Third, official bodies are appointed to hear and act upon complaints from citizens against the police.

Chapter Two

NATIONAL POLICE ORGANIZATIONS

Police organizations around the world form a wide spectrum: the national police forces of most countries in continental Europe represent extreme cases of the centralized model, and the police system of the United States represents the decentralized extreme. In between are hybrid cases, such as Canada. Although two provinces of Canada, Ontario and Quebec, have decentralized police systems, a single force, the Royal Canadian Mounted Police, has jurisdiction in the rest of the country. Police forces also may be classified as centralized or decentralized relative

Royal Canadian Mounted Police, armed with tear gas guns, patrol near the Bank of Canada building during an international financial meeting in Ottawa, Ontario. The building had been defaced during a demonstration.

to each other. For example, police organizations in the United Kingdom—including about fifty regional police forces in England, Scotland, and Wales—are generally considered decentralized, but when compared with the tens of thousands of police forces in the United States, they appear fairly centralized. However, the United Kingdom also has a domestic security service, MI5, that bridges the customary gap between intelligence gathering and criminal policing. Attempts to bridge that gap are a feature of more centralized policing systems.

ROYAL CANADIAN MOUNTED POLICE

The Royal Canadian Mounted Police (RCMP), also called the Mounties, is Canada's federal police force. It is also the provincial and criminal police establishment in all provinces except Ontario and Quebec and the only police force in the Yukon and Northwest territories. It is responsible for Canadian internal security as well.

Founded in 1873, it was originally called the North West Mounted Rifles, but the reaction of the United States to the idea of an armed force patrolling the border caused the name to be changed to the North West Mounted Police. The force's first installation was Fort McLeod, in the province of Alberta, and it was the only authority for 300,000 square miles (800,000 square kilometers) of wilderness. The original force of 300 men was sent to deal with traders from the United States who were creating havoc among the Indians by trading cheap whiskey for bison hides. With a combination of tact and dogged persistence, the Mounties succeeded in driving these men back across the border and pacifying the Indians. Their just treatment of the Indians resulted in the neutrality of the powerful Blackfoot Confederacy during the Riel Rebellion of 1885.

As the only authority in the region, the force assumed a wide variety of duties. Under its surveillance, the western extension of the Canadian Pacific Railway was completed in

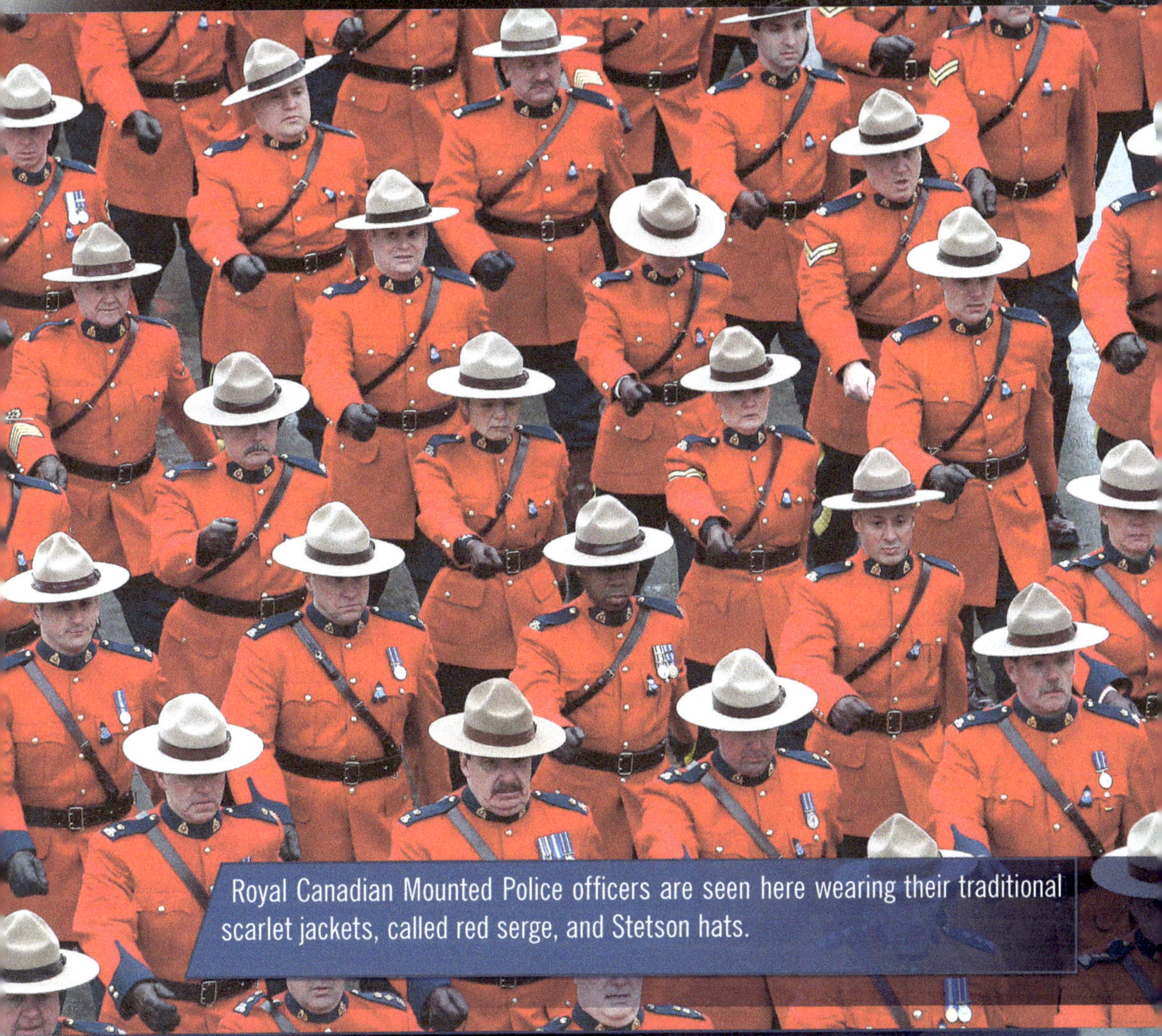

Royal Canadian Mounted Police officers are seen here wearing their traditional scarlet jackets, called red serge, and Stetson hats.

1885. Anticipating the gold rush of 1898, the Mounties preceded the first wave of prospectors to the Yukon. As more than 300,000 settlers poured into Canada after the turn of the twentieth century, the Mounties were of considerable assistance to those inexperienced in wilderness survival. In 1904, the prefix "Royal" was added to their name, and in 1920, when

(continued on the next page)

(continued from the previous page)

it became a federal force throughout Canada, the present name was adopted, and the headquarters were moved from Regina, Saskatchewan, to Ottawa, Ontario. In the 1930s, the marine and air divisions, the dog section, and the first of three crime-detection laboratories were added to the force.

The facilities of the national police service of the RCMP—crime-detection laboratories and the identification branch of the force—are available to all authorized police forces. The RCMP-sponsored Canadian Police College is attended by selected members of the force and outside forces. The RCMP is a member of the International Criminal Police Organization (Interpol).

CENTRALIZED POLICE ORGANIZATIONS

Western continental Europe favors the centralized model of policing, as do Russia and other Eastern European countries. However, there is considerable variation among the centralized police organizations of Western European countries. Most fall under one of four categories: (1) complete centralization in one police force; (2) high centralization, with a small number of national police forces; (3) regional centralization under federal authority; and (4) decentralized local policing, with a strong national agency. Other commonalities among

European police systems are a strong domestic security arm that is integrated partly or wholly into the system and unarmed municipal police forces that enforce various local bylaws and regulate traffic.

Sweden is an example of a country with a completely centralized police system. It has a single national police force, the Swedish Police Authority, which is part of the Ministry of Justice and led by the National Police Commissioner. It comprises seven police regions, which are further subdivided into police districts.

Swedish police officers patrol Stockholm's Arlanda Airport after terrorist attacks took place in Brussels, Belgium, in March 2016. Sweden has a centralized police force called the Swedish Police Authority.

France, Italy, and Spain exemplify the model of high centralization with a small number of national police forces. There are two national police agencies in France: the National Police and the National Gendarmerie. The National Police operates in cities, whereas the National Gendarmerie polices rural areas and small towns. A third force, the State Security Police (French: Compagnies Républicaines de Sécurité), is a part of the National Police but is organized like a military unit. Italy's national police agencies include the State Police, which is responsible for public order and security; the Carabinieri, which functions both as a military police force and as a civil police force; and the Financial Police, or Treasury Guard, which deals with economic crimes such as tax evasion and counterfeiting. Spain's police system consists of two national police agencies: the National Police, which is responsible for most police duties, and the Civil Guard, which is a militarized force that patrols rural areas and also specializes in the protection of national security (counterterrorism) and crowd control.

Germany and the Netherlands typify regional centralization under federal authority. Germany has two federal police forces: the Federal Criminal Police Office, whose role is similar to that of the Federal Bureau of Investigation (FBI) in the United States, and the Federal Police. However, the basic policing structure rests on the state or province police forces, which are similarly structured.

In the Netherlands, the National Police operates under the authority of the Ministry of Security and Justice, but the regional police forces provide the backbone of the policing system. There is also a military police force, the Royal Netherlands Constabulary (Dutch: Koninklijke Marechaussee), which polices the Dutch borders and provides security at airports, among other tasks.

The Belgian police system features a federal police force, which brought together the former gendarmerie and the national criminal investigation unit, and numerous local police forces, each of which is responsible to a mayor. Belgium's system of policing is closer to an Anglo-American decentralized model than the other European centralized models.

The police forces in Russia and the former Soviet-bloc countries of Eastern Europe entered a state of transition after the collapse of the Soviet Union in 1991. The Soviet Union was policed by a single centralized police force, the Militia, that operated in the various territorial divisions of the country under the rigid authority of the Ministry of the Interior (MVD). After the former Soviet republics gained independence, many of the constituent parts of the Militia also became fully independent, while other parts remained in the Russian Federation. The police forces within the states of the Russian Federation enjoy some independence from the federal government. Although much of the centralized police apparatus of the former Soviet Union is still in place, it

Belgian police officers patrol a street in Brussels during an operation at the home of a suspected terrorist in 2015. Belgium has a federal police force as well as a number of local forces.

is weaker; similar institutions in the former Soviet-bloc countries have also been weakened to varying degrees.

DECENTRALIZED POLICE ORGANIZATIONS

The United States has what may be the most decentralized police system in the world, characterized by an extraordinary degree of duplication and conflicting jurisdiction. Although every community is entitled to run its own police department, none can prevent federal or state officials from conducting local investigations into offenses over which they have jurisdiction. There are five major types of police agency: (1) the federal system, consisting of the Department of Homeland Security and the Department of Justice, including the FBI, the Drug Enforcement Administration, the Secret Service, the Postal Inspection Service, and many others; (2) police forces and criminal investigation agencies established by each of the fifty states; (3) sheriffs' departments in several thousand counties, plus a few county police forces that either duplicate the sheriffs' police jurisdictions or displace them; (4) the police forces of about 1,000 cities and more than 20,000 townships and New England towns; and (5) the police of some

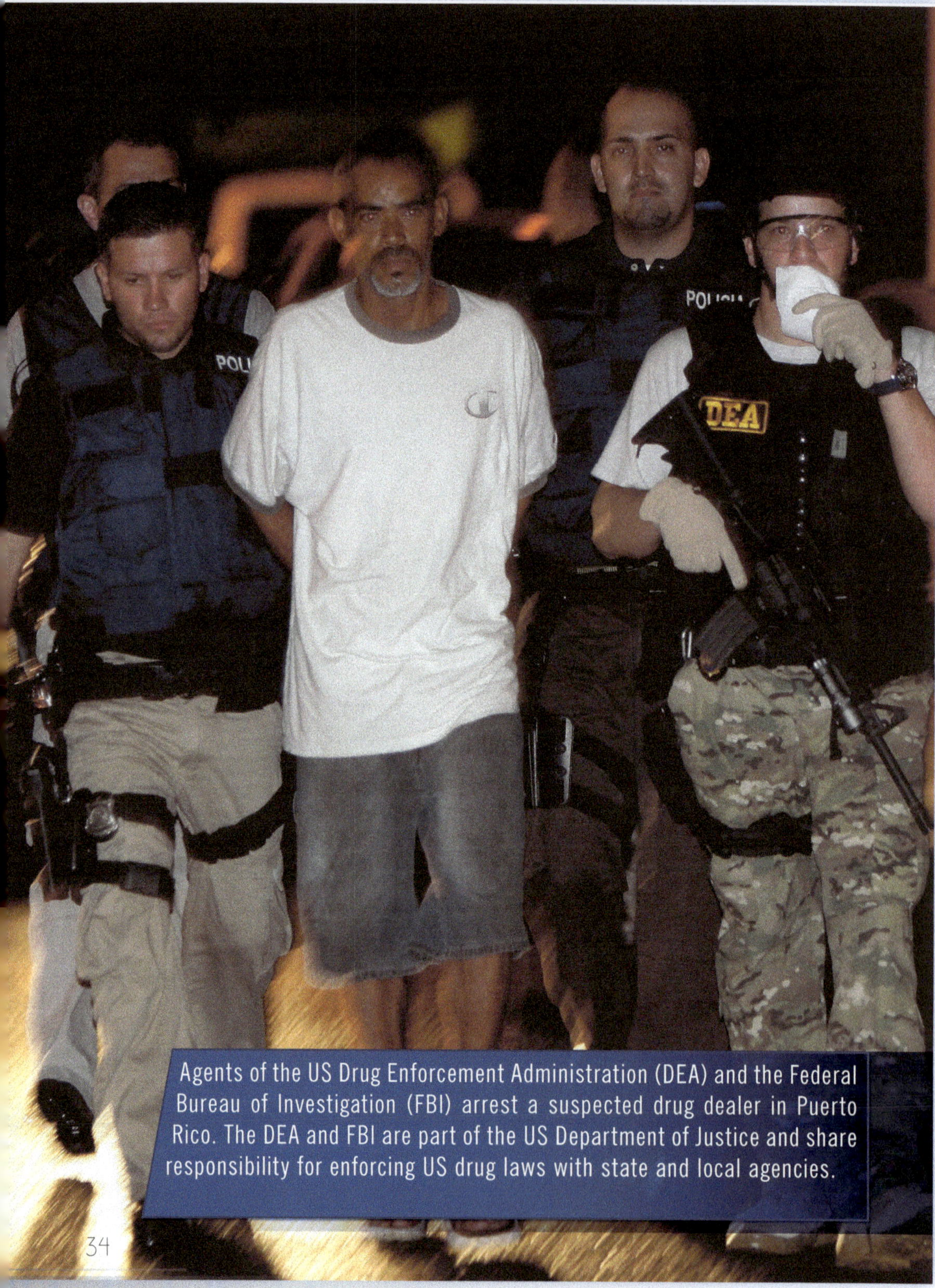

Agents of the US Drug Enforcement Administration (DEA) and the Federal Bureau of Investigation (FBI) arrest a suspected drug dealer in Puerto Rico. The DEA and FBI are part of the US Department of Justice and share responsibility for enforcing US drug laws with state and local agencies.

15,000 villages, boroughs, and incorporated towns. To this list must be added special categories, such as the police of the District of Columbia; various forces attached to authorities governing bridges, tunnels, and parks; university, or "campus," police forces; and some units that police special districts formed for fire protection, soil conservation, and other diverse purposes. Although there are tens of thousands of police forces throughout the United States, the majority of them consist of just a few officers.

The existing American police structure to some extent reflects public opposition to any concentration of police power. It has been argued that the nation would suffer, and local governments would be enfeebled, should all offenses become federal offenses and all police power be transferred to Washington, DC. Local problems require local remedies, according to this view. On the other hand, it has also been argued that the integration and consolidation of police forces would reduce costs and increase efficiency. As this debate continues, many small municipalities in the United States have chosen to maintain their own police forces, while others have joined together to form regional police departments.

Other countries with federal political structures have federal police forces as well as state forces that operate on the same principles as those observed in the United States. In Australia, for example, each of the six states has its own police force and its own laws but does

President Pranab Mukherjee of India (*second from left*) presents a sword of honor for the best outdoor officer trainee during a parade of the Indian Police Service at the National Police Academy in 2013.

not legislate in matters pertaining to federal organizations and cannot pass laws that conflict with those of the commonwealth. Yet even countries like Australia have attempted to move away from the fragmentation

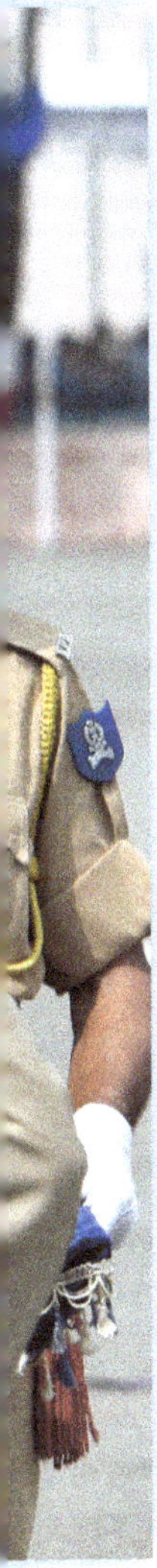

that is characteristic of American policing. The model that many countries have adopted blends strong central leadership with a limited number of regional police forces, as in the United Kingdom.

After India's accession to independence in 1947, the minister of home affairs, Vallabhbhai Jhaverbhai Patel, established the All-India Services for public administration. One of those services is the Indian Police Service, which trains officers for the police forces of the states and big cities, such as New Delhi and Mumbai (Bombay). Although police leaders are trained at least in part by the Indian Police Service, the various states and main cities have different police forces with their own specific features, making for a complex policing structure. India also has central security agencies, such as the Border Security Force, the Central Reserve Police Force, and the National Security Guard, which specialize in counterterrorism. Although they are national services, their members may be dispatched to particular areas to help solve local problems.

The police forces of Japan are deployed in a number of regional police prefectures. Each regional force has a certain degree of autonomy. The police operate out of small police posts—*koban* in cities and *chuzaisho* in rural areas—and maintain an unparalleled closeness to the communities they serve. The central government's National Police Agency exerts strong leadership over local police forces and promotes common standards;

it also engages in secret intelligence gathering. Japanese policing methods have been thoroughly studied by Western scholars and were influential in the development of community policing in Anglo-Saxon countries. Police ministations and storefronts, for example, were in part modeled on the *koban*.

The police system of Brazil, a federal state, also features a balance between a central authority and a limited number of regional police forces. The police force of each state is under the authority of the state's Secretariat for Public Security. Like many other countries of Latin America, Brazil also possesses a military police force that is controlled by the armed forces, as are the gendarmeries in Europe. Hence, although military police are deployed in the various Brazilian states, they report to the headquarters of the various military regions.

POLICE ORGANIZATIONS IN AFRICA

Because of political fragmentation and the disruption caused by numerous civil wars, it is difficult to give an account of policing in Africa. Enduring civil conflict has generated a breakdown of law and order in such countries as the Democratic Republic of the Congo and Somalia despite the nominal existence of policing organizations. In some countries, such as Nigeria, widespread police corruption fundamentally undermines attempts to bring justice to the population. In countries with very high rates of violent crime, such as South Africa, there is a massive resort to private policing of every kind.

A police officer in Musebeya, Rwanda, poses with his baton. The Rwanda National Police was established in 2000, combining the Gendarmerie Nationale, the Communal Police, and the Judicial Police Inspectors into one unit.

In fact, although many African countries have national police forces, policing functions are commonly performed by the private sector and sometimes by residents themselves. In addition, all countries in Africa depend to various extents on the military for the maintenance of order and for crisis intervention. They also have created national agencies responsible for state security.

European colonial powers established policing systems in both North Africa and sub-Saharan Africa, and the legacy of colonialism accounts for many differences in national policing systems on the continent. In Algeria, Morocco, Mauritania, and Tunisia, policing systems replicate the centralized police model applied in France, while Libya follows the centralized Italian model. The countries of West and Central Africa that were colonized by France, Belgium, and Germany also have centralized police systems. In general, the police forces in those countries have three parts, including an independent municipal police force for the capital city, a national police force for all other cities, and a militarized gendarmerie for the countryside. Countries that fell under the British sphere of influence, such as Egypt and Kenya, tend to have less-centralized police systems, with both regional police forces and municipal police organizations in large cities. Unlike other former British colonies, South Africa is policed by a single force—the South African Police Service (SAPS)—which conducts criminal investigations, intelligence, and forensics at the national level and is also deployed in the provinces of the country. Whether operating at the national or provincial levels, SAPS is under the command of a single national commissioner. These generalizations on policing in Africa allow for other exceptions as well; for instance, Eritrea, Ethiopia, and Uganda developed their own mixtures of federal (centralized) and regional (decentralized) policing in the postcolonial era.

Chapter Three

POLICE WORK AND LAW ENFORCEMENT

The activities of police forces are adapted to the kinds of societies in which they operate. Some common features of police work in different societies are the result of similar technologies. Yet within the same society—and sometimes even within the same police force—there may be variations. One police administrator, because of his or her personal beliefs or because of his or her perception of public opinion, may allocate more resources to certain types of crime or to certain police duties than to others. Thus, police officers in different neighborhoods may develop different patterns of policing.

Within the framework of enforcement policy, police work is divided into various branches. The largest

A police officer uses a radar gun to check a vehicle's speed in New Haven, Connecticut. Uniformed patrol officers typically enforce traffic laws; investigate collisions, complaints, and disturbances; serve warrants; and write reports, among other duties.

number of officers is usually allocated to uniformed patrol, either on foot or with motor transport. Studies of the activities of police on patrol indicate that only a small portion of their time goes to making arrests

or initiating formal actions under criminal law. Moreover, whether one considers the types of calls for service that police receive, the calls to which police are dispatched, or the activities that police initiate on their own, it is clear that the majority of police activities consist of providing emergency services, maintaining order, resolving disputes, and providing other services.

POLICE AND COURTS

One of the most important ways in which police are held accountable for the manner in which they perform their duties is through the courts. In France (and in countries with similar legal procedures, such as Italy), police officers making inquiries are under the direction of an investigating magistrate. The supervision exercised by the magistrate is minimal in the vast majority of cases. The police conduct their inquiries with a large degree of independence and are generally successful in closing investigations by obtaining confessions from suspects. Investigating magistrates play an important role only in high-profile investigations, such as those directed at political corruption,

Police officers and magistrates in Palermo, Italy, appear with jewelry, coins, and watches recovered from a criminal who had hidden the valuables under the floor of an apartment. In Italy, magistrates direct police investigations.

economic crime, organized crime, and terrorism. The British and American common-law procedure is in principle different, as there is no equivalent of the investigating magistrate, but the institution of the grand jury plays a similar role. The grand jury works with the prosecution, which has the investigative services of the police at its disposal.

Once a case is brought to court, the proceedings are not as different between the two systems as legal terminology suggests. (The Anglo-Saxon procedure is called adversarial or accusatorial, whereas the procedure in continental Europe is called inquisitorial.) In both traditions, the accused is presumed innocent, and the judge (and a jury in jury trials) listens to the prosecution's argument and its evidence that the accused has broken a particular law, as well as to arguments to the contrary presented by the defense. The judge or jury reaches a verdict, and the defendant, if convicted, is sentenced.

If the accusatorial system is to function justly in Anglo-Saxon countries, the police must bring all cases of lawbreaking before the courts. It is for the court to decide whether punishment is merited. In practice, however, the police exercise considerable discretion as to whom they will prosecute. Three chief arguments favor police discretion in this area. First, it has proved impossible to draft and keep up-to-date a criminal code that unambiguously encompasses all conduct intended to be deemed criminal; for example, there are technical offenses or offenses that public opinion no longer regards as criminal. Second, because those charged with enforcing the law do not have sufficient resources to enforce all the laws all the time, enforcement must be selective. Third, bringing to court a person who has only technically violated a law may, in practice, unduly damage that person's reputation.

The courts control police activities in other ways. In Britain, for example, codes of practice established by the Police and Criminal Evidence Act 1984 (PACE) outline safeguards for accused persons while they are under investigation. If it can be proved in court that the police failed to warn a person properly that he

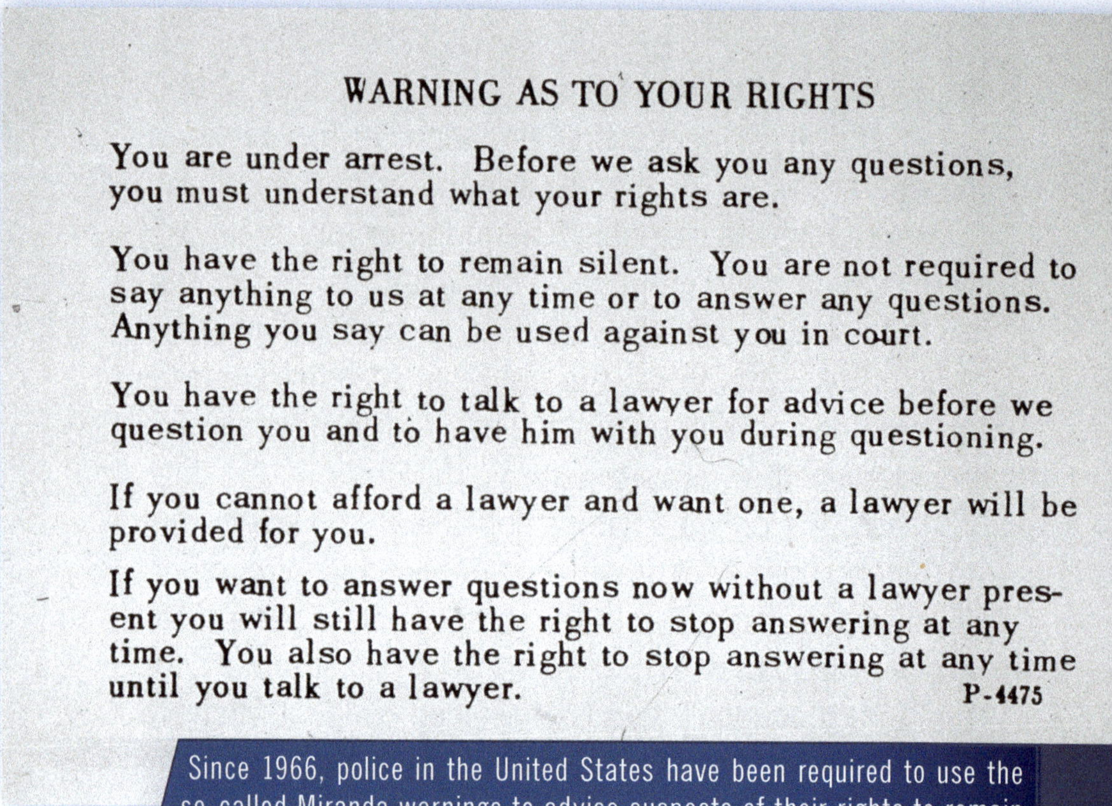

WARNING AS TO YOUR RIGHTS

You are under arrest. Before we ask you any questions, you must understand what your rights are.

You have the right to remain silent. You are not required to say anything to us at any time or to answer any questions. Anything you say can be used against you in court.

You have the right to talk to a lawyer for advice before we question you and to have him with you during questioning.

If you cannot afford a lawyer and want one, a lawyer will be provided for you.

If you want to answer questions now without a lawyer present you will still have the right to stop answering at any time. You also have the right to stop answering at any time until you talk to a lawyer. P-4475

Since 1966, police in the United States have been required to use the so-called Miranda warnings to advise suspects of their rights to remain silent and to have a lawyer present during questioning.

was under suspicion of having committed a particular offense and that any statement he made could be used as evidence against him, then the prosecution might fail. In a celebrated case (*Miranda v. Arizona*), the US Supreme Court ruled in 1966 that accused persons must be informed by the police of their right not to answer police questions and to consult a lawyer before questioning; accused persons are also entitled to assigned counsel (also called public defenders), paid

MIRANDA V. ARIZONA

The US Supreme Court's ruling in *Miranda v. Arizona* specified a code of conduct for police interrogations of criminal suspects held in custody. With this decision the court reversed an Arizona court's conviction of Ernesto Miranda on charges of kidnapping and rape. After having been identified in a police lineup, Miranda was questioned by police; he confessed and then signed a written statement without first having been told that he had the right to have a lawyer present to advise him or that he had the right to remain silent. Miranda's confession was later used at his trial to obtain his conviction. The court held that the prosecution could not use his statements obtained by the police while the suspect was in custody unless the police had complied with several procedural safeguards to secure the Fifth Amendment privilege against self-incrimination. These safeguards, which remain in place today, are known as the Miranda warnings.

for by the public, if they cannot afford to hire a lawyer. In other decisions, police have been prevented from submitting at a trial any evidence that was obtained by unreasonable search and seizure.

POLICE AND MINORITIES

The relationships between police and ethnic and racial minorities present some of the more enduring and complex problems in policing throughout the world. Such relationships can be harmonious, but they are often problematic. For example, minorities may be generally deprived of police protection and other services to which they are entitled. More specifically, police may refrain from addressing criminal behavior (for example, domestic violence) within a particular minority group because they believe that members of that group typically engage in such behavior. A more acute problem is direct conflict between police and minorities. On the part of police, conflict may take the form of harassment, brutality, or excessive enforcement.

Although it is no excuse for lack of fairness, police attitudes toward minorities reflect the values of the larger community. When the community is hostile toward a particular minority group, police may feel that discriminatory behavior toward that group is justified. Police even may aggravate an existing prejudice, though they seldom generate prejudice on their own.

A police officer arrests a demonstrator during a protest in August 2015 marking the one-year anniversary of the shooting of unarmed African American teenager Michael Brown by a white police officer in Ferguson, Missouri. The shooting and its aftermath sparked a national debate about race and police treatment of minorities.

The intensity of community and police prejudice against minority groups depends on historical and social factors. The longer a minority has been seen as inferior, the more likely it is to be discriminated against.

Such groups may include nomads (such as the Roma in Europe), indigenous peoples in former European colonies, or smaller tribes in societies where tribal membership is socially significant. A war or a warlike situation can provoke hostility toward certain immigrant groups or other minorities perceived as the "enemy": Japanese Americans were treated in this way during World War II, as were many Muslims in Western countries after the September 11 terrorist attacks in the United States in 2001. Police discrimination may also occur when the majority of a society perceives a minority group as refusing to endorse the majority's values. For instance, the inferior status of women in some immigrant communities in Western countries has created considerable hostility toward the men in those communities. Finally, circumstantial resentment plays an important part in discrimination against minorities. For example, immigrant workers who were welcomed by the majority when work was plentiful may be the target of harassment in periods of unemployment.

Recruitment policies that determine the racial and ethnic makeup of a police force can significantly affect the relationships between the police and minorities. Although it is no guarantee of harmony, it is desirable that the racial and ethnic composition of the force reflect that of the larger community. However, that goal is often difficult to achieve. For instance, in large American cities such as Chicago, Illinois, significant segments of the Hispanic minority speak only Spanish, which precludes their being recruited by the police. The worst-case scenario occurs when the whole police organization is made up of members of a community that is in open conflict with another group. That was the case in the United States during the segregation of African Americans in the South—some police officers were actually members of racist organizations such as the Ku Klux Klan. It was also the case in the late 1960s in Northern Ireland, where despite a provision that the Royal Ulster Constabulary (RUC) recruit one-third of its members from among Ulster Catholics, the proportion of Catholics in the force was much smaller than that. The RUC was severely criticized for its brutality in policing the Catholic civil rights marches in 1968–69. The bias in police recruitment was even worse in South Africa under the system of racial segregation called apartheid, when the police forces were all-white organizations that frequently abused their power in dealings with black South Africans.

Today, although troublesome relationships between police and minorities remain common, police are increasingly aware of such problems and have taken broad steps to solve them. The community-policing reforms of the late twentieth century, for example, were motivated in part by the desire to reduce conflict with minorities. However, improvements can happen only in societies in which there is police accountability. Without

accountability, complaints about police actions may be met with severe reprisals, including the killing of complainants by police officers.

CROWDS AND RIOTS

Group violence is one of the most difficult problems of policing. Riots have played a role both in the creation of police forces and in their reform. For instance, frequent and serious rioting in Britain during the eighteenth century, such as the anti-Catholic Gordon riots of 1780, left a lasting impression on police reformers. The subsequent Peterloo Massacre of 1819, in which cavalry killed eleven protesters and injured several hundred during a radical political rally, helped to spur the British government to create the London Metropolitan Police in 1829. Riots also had played a considerable part in the creation of the French police in 1666. By the end of the twentieth century, however, many police forces were coming under increasing criticism for their often brutal methods of controlling crowds.

Police equipped with riot gear in Athens, Greece, confront farmers protesting a new government economic policy.

TYPES OF MASS EVENTS

Crowds that have the potential to become violent form for various reasons, including planned political protests; such crowds may also gather spontaneously. The nature of the mass event to be policed determines what kinds of police tactics may or may not succeed.

In democratic countries, political demonstrations have several common features. They are generally structured events, and the courses of marches are often predetermined and negotiated with the police. Political protests that occur in the context of international events—for example, political summits and meetings of global economic bodies such as the World Trade Organization—differ from national or local political protests in one respect that is important for policing: they bring together groups of protesters that may have different aims. Some groups simply may want their message to be heard; others may aim to disrupt the meeting as much as possible. Although the police may come to an understanding with some protesters, others may generate confrontations despite any attempts at negotiations. Thus, a great deal of group violence may accompany meetings of international bodies, as was the case at the Asia-Pacific Economic Cooperation summit in Vancouver, British Columbia, in 1997; the World Trade Organization meeting in Seattle, Washington, in 1999; and the European Union summit in Gothenburg, Sweden, in 2001.

Still, political protests and other events that are planned in advance tend to have less potential for violence than spontaneous gatherings. In many cases, riots occur against a backdrop of long-smoldering frustration

A Canadian police officer throws a tear gas canister into a crowd of rioters during the Third Summit of the Americas meeting in Quebec city, Quebec, in 2001. Group violence frequently occurs during meetings of international bodies.

and anger—for example, over racial or ethnic discrimination—and are triggered by a single controversial event. Riots in Los Angeles, California, in 1992, for example, were sparked by the acquittal of two police officers on charges stemming from their beating of an African American motorist, and in 2005 riots broke out in France (in large suburbs mainly populated by immigrants) after two youths of North African origin were accidentally killed while allegedly running from police.

METHODS OF CROWD POLICING

Four basic types of organization may police crowds: military forces, paramilitary forces, militarized police units, and unspecialized police forces. These organizations use primarily two strategies: escalated force and negotiated management.

In many countries, excepting Western-style democracies, the military, rather than the police, performs crowd control. There are many variants of this model, which differ primarily according to the level of force the military is willing to use. In some countries ruled by dictatorships, such as Iraq under Saddam Hussein, the whole might of the army, including the air force, has been used to quash any kind of public demonstration against the regime. Other countries in Asia, Africa, and Central and South America also leave crowd control to the military, though limited resources may prevent the military from mobilizing sophisticated weapons or vast numbers of soldiers. Even in Western democratic countries, governments increasingly call on the military to police crowds, especially in disaster situations—such as the US city of New Orleans, Louisiana, following Hurricane

In Munich, Germany, police officers armed with machine guns guard a street near a train station after officials obtained intelligence suggesting the possibility of a terrorist attack.

Katrina in 2005—and in situations in which rioters are heavily armed.

In some countries, such as Germany, Italy, and France, paramilitary forces within the centralized police

THE MILITARIZATION OF THE POLICE IN THE UNITED STATES

Beginning in the early 1980s, police forces in the United States increasingly used weapons, armor, tactics, and vehicles that were once reserved for the battlefield. The model for today's SWAT team began in Los Angeles in the late 1960s. At that time, the Los Angeles Police Department (LAPD) created the first specialized force of highly trained officers who could use overwhelming force and violence to defuse emergency situations in which lives were at immediate risk—incidents involving active shooters, bank robberies, riots, and hostage scenarios.

After a series of high-profile raids in the late 1960s and early 1970s against groups such as the Black Panthers and the Symbionese Liberation Army, the SWAT idea gained momentum. By 1975, the number of SWAT teams in the United States had soared from one to more than five hundred. During the 1970s, SWAT teams were reserved for emergency situations in which lives were at risk, but by the early 1980s, the use of militarized weapons and tactics was becoming more widespread as part of the US "war on drugs." During the 1990s, the US Department of Defense began transferring millions of pieces of military equipment—including machine guns, grenade launchers, armored personnel carriers, tanks, and helicopters—to federal, state, and local law-enforcement agencies. This program sparked a

SWAT team members ride on an armored car as they search for an armed suspect in Los Angeles, California. The militarization of US police forces has been a hotly debated issue.

massive increase in the number of SWAT teams. By 2005, four-fifths of towns with populations of 25,000–50,000 had a SWAT team.

Some observers argued that with the adoption of a soldier's gear, tactics, and training, certain police departments had also adopted a soldier's mind-set. Supporters claimed that the practice was necessary to confront increasingly well-armed criminals as well as the twenty-first-century threat of terrorism. Critics said that domestic police and the military were distinct institutions with fundamentally different roles and that conflating the two posed a grave threat to civil liberties.

system are charged with policing crowds. In France, for example, the State Security Police (a component of the National Police) specializes in order maintenance and crowd control. In democratic Anglo-Saxon countries, militarized police units embedded within a police force are a common instrument of policing crowds; all large police forces in those countries have such units. Some of their members are officially assigned to other units (such as patrol) and are called upon only in cases of emergency. Militarized police units bear various names, such as special weapons and tactics teams (SWAT teams), but their methods of training and operation, as well as their equipment and firepower, are similar.

Small police forces cannot afford special units and have to police crowds on their own. In crisis situations, they generally fare badly, as did the municipal forces in various parts of the United States during the 1960s and 1970s when civil rights and Vietnam War protests were frequent.

The most ancient strategy of crowd control, escalated force (the use of increasing amounts of force until the crowd disperses), still prevails in most countries that have not adopted Western-style democracy. Even in democracies, however, escalated force was the traditional way of controlling crowds until the 1970s, when the strategy of negotiated management emerged. The success of the latter strategy depends on two key factors: the willingness of the police and the groups involved to negotiate control of the event and, more fundamentally, the availability of group representatives with whom to negotiate. Such people are easily found in cases of domestic political protests and labor unrest, which naturally involve political and union leaders. In the case of international protests, however, negotiating control requires the cooperation of all the groups involved. In general, the greater the perceived threat to the controlling party, the less inclined it will be to negotiate, particularly if the force that it can summon is overwhelming. Although many scholars of policing expected that the strategy of negotiated management would gradually replace the strategy of escalation of force in Western-style democracies, their belief was belied by numerous violent confrontations between police and protesters at various international meetings held in democratic countries at the beginning of the twenty-first century.

Meanwhile, a third strategy of crowd control, called command and control, emerged in the United States. Spearheaded by the New York City Police Department, the strategy was basically an updated version of the escalation of force method, with advanced technological underpinnings. The strategy involves the fragmentation of crowds before they may become rioting mobs and the tight control by police of public spaces allocated to demonstrators. Police may install large concrete and metal barriers, thereby establishing zones where protesters cannot congregate and organize. They may also disperse crowds with nonlethal weapons—for example, tear gas and rubber bullets. In addition, police may use electronic surveillance to monitor a crowd's size and movements, and they may make preemptive arrests of protest leaders or potential troublemakers.

Chapter Four

INTERNATIONAL POLICE ORGANIZATIONS AND HIGH POLICING

The leading police body at the international level is the International Criminal Police Organization, or Interpol. Officially launched in 1946, it included 190 member countries as of 2016. Other organizations also merge the police assets of multiple countries. For example, the European Police Office (Europol) is the European Union's law-enforcement arm. In addition, agencies devoted to the national security of different countries share intelligence for common security purposes. Police work aimed at the protection of national security is sometimes called high policing.

INTERPOL

Interpol, first known as the International Criminal Police Commission (ICPC), was founded in 1923 in Vienna, Austria, by the city's head of police, Johann Schober. Vienna had been the seat of the Austro-Hungarian Empire, which had maintained an extensive system of police files. The Nazis took over the ICPC in 1938, when Germany annexed Austria, but the organization's operations stopped with the outbreak of World War II. After the war, at a conference held in Brussels, Belgium, in 1946, the organization was reconstituted as Interpol, with headquarters in Paris, France (since 1989 in Lyon, France). Interpol's present constitution was ratified in 1956.

Each of Interpol's member countries has a bureau that maintains close contact with the organization's General Secretariat. The bureaus transmit criminal information that may be of interest to other countries. Within their own countries, they undertake inquiries, searches, and arrests requested by other countries and take steps to implement resolutions voted on by the annual assembly. Interpol also maintains and develops databases of fingerprints, DNA records, photographs, and other information that might be useful in tracking down criminals. Crimes of particular concern for Interpol are trafficking in human beings, transboundary

Headquartered in Lyon, France, Interpol is the world's largest international police organization. As of 2016, it had 190 member countries.

financial and organized crime, and international terrorism. In 2015, it opened the Interpol Global Complex for Innovation in Singapore to help combat cybercrime and other threats involving technology.

Interpol's effectiveness is limited by the fact that it resulted from a practical agreement between police forces rather than from an official convention between states. Interpol can act only within the framework of national laws; criminals can be returned only if an extradition treaty is in force and the offender is a citizen of the country requesting return. Moreover, because

Interpol's operations depend crucially on the exchange of intelligence, countries that cannot afford efficient intelligence databases cannot contribute significantly to the organization.

OTHER INTERNATIONAL POLICE FORCES

In the early twenty-first century, Interpol was no longer the only international policing organization. Police cooperation between members of the European Union

THE SCHENGEN AGREEMENT

The Schengen Agreement is an international convention initially approved by Belgium, France, West Germany (later Germany), Luxembourg, and the Netherlands in Schengen, Luxembourg, on June 14, 1985. The signatories agreed to begin reducing internal border controls, with the ultimate goal of allowing free movement of people between countries within the Schengen area. To implement this, a system of shared policies regarding visa and asylum applications was adopted by member countries, and a massive database, known as the Schengen Information System (SIS), was created to share information about people and goods moving within the Schengen zone.

Austrian foreign minister Ursula Plassnik (*left*) participates with other Austrians in the opening of a barrier at the Karavanke tunnel checkpoint between Austria and Slovenia on December 21, 2007.

By the time the agreement went into effect in March 1995, Italy, Spain, Portugal, and Greece had joined the original five members, with Austria, Denmark, Finland, Iceland, Norway, and Sweden following soon after. Although the Schengen Agreement originated outside the framework of the European Union, the Treaty of Amsterdam brought it into the body of EU law in 1999. Upgrades were made to the SIS to aid national law-enforcement bodies. In 2007, the Schengen area expanded to include the Czech Republic, Estonia, Hungary, Latvia, Lithuania, Malta, Poland, Slovakia, and Slovenia. The area was further enlarged by the addition of Switzerland the following year and Liechtenstein in 2011.

(EU), for example, was rapidly developing on the basis of various pieces of transnational legislation enacted by the European Parliament, including agreements and conventions against terrorism, drug trafficking, trafficking in human beings, money laundering, and organized crime. European police forces, which had participated in Interpol since its inception, increased their cooperation in 1975 with the launch of a counterterrorist initiative known as the TREVI group (TREVI being the French acronym for "terrorism, radicalism, extremism, and international violence"). The Schengen Agreement (1985), which allowed freedom of movement between the signatory countries, provided for further coordination between European police forces.

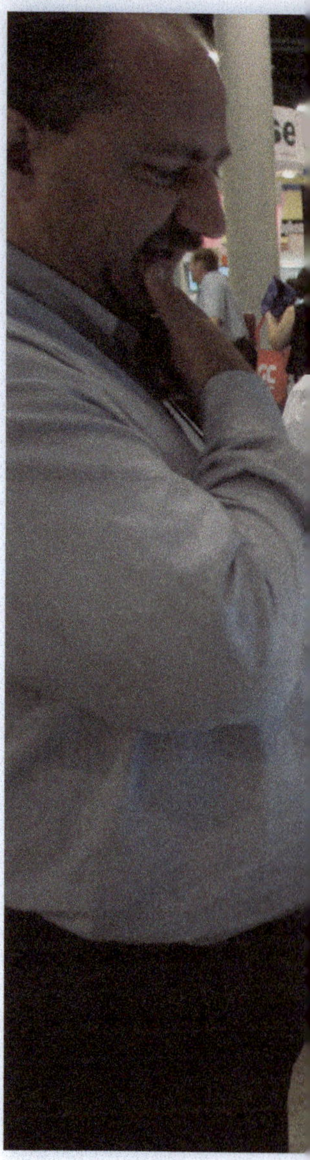

Europol, established in 1992 as the European Drugs Unit, supports the law-enforcement agencies of all countries in the EU by gathering and analyzing intelligence about members or possible members of international criminal organizations. Headquartered in The Hague in the Netherlands, Europol is far removed from police field operations. Its priority is building trust between the many law-enforcement organizations with which it works.

The International Association of Chiefs of Police (IACP) holds an annual conference. Here, IACP members review computerized touch-table satellite technology for possible acquisition by their departments.

The International Association of Chiefs of Police, with headquarters near Washington, DC, draws its members largely from the United States and is the leading voice in the United States for professional police standards.

It is active in training, research, and public relations. The International Police Association was founded in Britain in 1950 as a social organization. Although it is most active in Europe, its members come from dozens of countries worldwide. The association grants scholarships for study abroad and travel and arranges annual conferences.

HIGH POLICING: THE PROTECTION OF NATIONAL SECURITY

In continental Europe, police work that is directed at protecting national security is known as high policing, in reference to the "higher" interests of the state. There is no conventional designation for this category of policing in Anglo-Saxon countries, however. Calling it "secret" or "political" policing would be too vague, as all police work is to a certain extent both secret (police generally do not reveal their methods until a case is completed) and political (police enforce laws determined by the political system in power). Furthermore, the term "secret police" is usually used to refer to clandestine and extralegal organizations like the Gestapo of the Nazis, whose main functions are to eliminate opponents of the regime and to make the population passive through intimidation and terror.

Whatever it may be called, high policing in Anglo-Saxon countries is performed by both national police forces and specialized agencies. Among them are the FBI and the Secret Service in the United States, MI5 in the United Kingdom, the Australian Security Intelligence Organisation, the Canadian Security Intelligence Service, and the New Zealand Security Intelligence Service. These organizations usually confront domestic or internal threats to national security, whereas the military or military-intelligence agencies generally handle foreign or external threats. This distinction can become

US Secret Service agents stand guard at a presidential campaign event in 2016. Besides their duties investigating counterfeiting and protecting presidents, their families, and other national leaders and visiting dignitaries, Secret Service agents also guard major presidential and vice presidential candidates within 120 days of a general election.

USA PATRIOT ACT

The USA PATRIOT Act—in full, the Uniting and Strengthening America by Providing Appropriate Tools Required to Intercept and Obstruct Terrorism Act of 2001—was passed by the US Congress in response to the September 11, 2001, terrorist attacks and signed into law by President George W. Bush in October 2001. Also called the PATRIOT Act, the law significantly expanded the search and surveillance powers of federal law-enforcement and intelligence agencies.

Some key provisions of the legislation consisted of amendments to the Wiretap Act, which had prohibited eavesdropping by the government on private face-to-face, telephone, and electronic communications except as authorized by court order in narrowly defined circumstances in cases of serious crimes. Sections 201 and 202 of the USA PATRIOT Act added computer and terrorist crimes to the list of serious offenses in connection with which law-enforcement officials could seek a court order to conduct eavesdropping. Section 209 established that voice mail was not entitled to the same protections that governed telephone conversations but only to the weaker safeguards applicable to telephone records and email stored with third parties (usually an internet service provider).

Section 216 permitted the use of trap-and-trace devices and pen registers—which record the source and destination, respectively, of calls made to and from a particular telephone—to monitor electronic communications,

On October 26, 2001, US president George W. Bush signed the USA PATRIOT Act in the East Room of the White House.

understood to include email and internet browsing. Court orders for such surveillance did not require probable cause (a showing of facts that would lead a reasonable person to believe that the surveillance would be likely to uncover evidence of criminal activity by the target) but only a certification by the government that the information sought was likely to be relevant to a criminal investigation. Section 206 of the act permitted the government to authorize "roving" electronic surveillance, which could be carried out in any location and with any equipment.

(continued on the next page)

(continued from the previous page)

In 2015, the USA Freedom Act was passed by Congress and signed into law by President Barack Obama. This law restored and revised some provisions of the PATRIOT Act that had recently expired. For example, the USA Freedom Act set limits on the collection of US citizens' telecommunications data by US intelligence agencies, particularly the National Security Agency.

blurred, however, especially in cases involving terrorism. For example, after the September 11 attacks of 2001, José Padilla, a US citizen accused of being an al-Qaeda operative, was arrested by the FBI but detained by the US military as an "enemy combatant."

The primary tool of high policing is intelligence, which is derived from both human and technological sources, the latter including electronic surveillance and eavesdropping. In the former country of East Germany, the Stasi, the state secret police agency, relied on vast numbers of informers for intelligence on the activities of East German citizens. The extent of the cooperation it obtained was so great that it tore the social fabric of the country apart when the agency's files were opened to the public after the fall of the Berlin Wall in 1989. In the United States, the USA PATRIOT Act of 2001 allowed for expanded domestic electronic surveillance of both US citizens and foreign residents, including by means of roving wiretaps and the seizure of voice-mail messages. In a provision that maintained the traditional high-policing function of monitoring the circulation of ideas in society, the PATRIOT Act also allowed law-enforcement and intelligence agencies to obtain the library borrowing records of individuals without their knowledge.

Because organizations involved in high policing tend to be granted extensive legal powers, there is a tendency, even in democratic countries, for such organizations to abuse their powers or even to operate outside the law. In some countries, for example, high-policing organizations regularly engage in actions of dubious legality, such as detaining people without charge, without legal representation, and without means of communication; some high-policing forces also engage in torture. In the worst cases, high policing becomes a substitute for the whole criminal justice system: suspects are arrested, tried, convicted, and sentenced by a national security agency, usually very quickly and in complete secrecy.

Concerns about the possibility of such abuses in the United States and Canada prompted many investigations into the national security services of those countries in the 1960s and later. A report commissioned by the Canadian government in 1966 supported these concerns, concluding that "a security service will inevitably be involved in actions that may contravene the spirit

if not the letter of the law, and with clandestine and other activities which may sometimes seem to infringe on [an] individual's rights." In the early twenty-first century, particularly in the period that followed the September 11 attacks, some US citizens were held in preventive detention in jails, and many foreign nationals were imprisoned without charge at the US naval base at Guantánamo Bay, Cuba. Some critics, including the United Nations, claimed that the interrogation techniques used on prisoners at Guantánamo amounted to torture.

The worst high-policing abuses occur in countries ruled by authoritarian or totalitarian regimes. High-policing organizations in such countries tend to have the following characteristics in common. First, they are accountable not to elected officials but only to the executive power. Second, they possess, and in fact are dominated by, a large military wing. Third, the military wings maintain their own penal administration and control a network of detention facilities (most often concentration camps). Fourth, these organizations systematically resort to torture, which is applied without concern for the human rights or even the lives of the victims.

The wide extent of such practices should not be taken to show that protecting national security requires violations of human rights. On the contrary, in most

US military personnel escort a detainee from Afghanistan to an interrogation center at the US naval base at Guantánamo Bay, Cuba. After the September 11 terrorist attacks on the United States, there was worldwide concern that some US interrogation methods were equivalent to torture.

democratic countries, the conduct of high policing, when subject to proper oversight, does not contradict democratic values or infringe upon basic civil or human rights.

Forms of policing have been used for thousands of years in many cultures. Ancient magistrates in eastern Asia appointed officers to enforce their authority. The early Greeks used slaves to arrest criminals and maintain order at public gatherings. In the Middle Ages,

A patrol officer in Utah performs a traffic stop while wearing a body camera that is attached to his eyeglasses. Many believe such cameras will assist in police accountability and help improve both the police's and the public's behavior during encounters.

some countries designated constables and marshals, who created small police forces.

In England, by the time of King Charles II (1630–1685), the government had a well-developed espionage system, while "thieftakers" chased down criminals. The king offered a large reward to "officers of justice" as well as citizens for apprehending "any Robber or High-way-man." Across the Atlantic, unpaid night watchmen were organized in colonial Boston and New York at about the same time. By the 1830s, major American cities were establishing full-time, paid police forces. On the western frontier, the Texas Rangers became the precursor of state police in 1835.

Today, police officers in most countries are highly trained. Many undertake extensive, specialized training for certain tasks. As the objectives, tactics, and weapons used by criminals have advanced, police tactics and equipment have become more modernized. Observers keep close watch to ensure that while police protect society against mounting threats, civil liberties are protected as well.

TIMELINE

1215 King John of England agrees to the Magna Carta. The thirty-ninth article of this document contains the first expression of the due process idea.

1631 Watchmen are organized in colonial Boston.

1647 Watchmen are organized in colonial New Amsterdam (later New York City).

1651 Watchmen are organized in Quebec City, Quebec.

1666 King Louis XIV of France issues an edict establishing the office of lieutenant of police.

1786 The Dublin Police Act creates a professional police force in Dublin, Ireland.

1791 The Fifth Amendment to the US Constitution is ratified, providing that "No person shall... be deprived of life, liberty, or property, without due process of law."

1800 Under Napoleon Bonaparte, Minister of Police Joseph Fouché reorganizes the French police.

1811 Tsar Alexander I creates the Russian Ministry of Police based on the French model.

1829 The Metropolitan Police Act is passed in England, establishing the London Metropolitan Police Department.

1835 Toronto, Ontario, creates a police department.

1838 Quebec city establishes a police department.

1840 Montreal, Quebec, creates a police department.

1844 The first police department in the United

States is established in New York City.
The Civil Guard of Spain, a paramilitary national police force, is created.

1857 The New York City Police Department establishes a detective unit.

1861 The Chicago Police Department establishes a detective unit.
The Carabinieri, an Italian national police force, becomes part of the Italian armed forces.

1865 The US Secret Service is established as a division of the Department of the Treasury to fight counterfeiting of US currency.

1870 The US Department of Justice is established.

1873 The North West Mounted Police (later renamed the Royal Canadian Mountain Police) is created to police western Canada.

1901 The US Secret Service permanently assumes the role of chief protective service for the president and other national leaders, their families, and visiting dignitaries.

1905 Pennsylvania establishes the first modern state police department.

1908 The Bureau of Investigation (later the Federal Bureau of Investigation, FBI) is established in the United States.

1909 The intelligence agency MI5 is formed in the United Kingdom to identify and counteract German spies who were working in Britain.

1910 The first crime laboratory is established in Lyon, France.

1913 The Judges' Rules are drawn up in Great Britain to outline safeguards for accused people while they are under investigation. These were later replaced by the codes of practice established by the Police and Criminal Evidence Act 1984 (PACE).

1923 The International Criminal Police Commission, now known as Interpol, is founded in Vienna, Austria.

1944 The State Security Police, a special mobile French police force, is created. It is now part of the National Police.

1947 The US Central Intelligence Agency (CIA) is created under the National Security Act.

1948 The Indian Police Service is formed as part of the All-India Services.

1965 Sweden's Rikspolis is established as a national police force.

1966 The US Supreme Court case *Miranda v. Arizona* results in a ruling specifying a code of conduct for police interrogations of criminal suspects held in custody.

Late 1960s Special weapons and tactics (SWAT) teams are first developed in the Los Angeles Police Department.

1979 The Australian Federal Police is created.

1985 The Schengen Agreement is signed, reducing

border controls between the participating countries and creating the Schengen Information System (SIS) to share information about people and goods moving within the Schengen zone.

1986 The National Police is established in Spain.

2000 The Carabinieri, previously considered part of the army, becomes an independent branch of the Italian armed forces.

2001 Following the September 11 terrorist attacks against the United States, President George W. Bush creates the Office of Homeland Security to coordinate counterterrorism efforts by federal, state, and local law-enforcement agencies. President Bush signs the USA PATRIOT Act into law.

2003 The US Department of Homeland Security is established.

2015 The Swedish Police Authority replaces the Rikspolis as the national police authority in Sweden.

GLOSSARY

ACCOUNTABILITY An obligation or willingness to accept responsibility or to account for one's actions.

AGGRIEVED Having a grievance, especially having suffered from unfair treatment or denial of legal rights.

APARTHEID A policy of racial segregation and discrimination practiced in South Africa in the second half of the twentieth century.

AUTHORITARIAN Relating to or favoring a concentration of power in a leader or an elite not constitutionally responsible to the people.

COMMON LAW The body of laws that developed from English court decisions and customs and that form the basis of laws in the United States.

CONFLATING Bringing together.

COUNTERTERRORISM The actions taken by governments and military and police forces to prevent terrorist attacks and destroy terrorist networks.

CYBERCRIME Criminal activity (such as fraud or identity theft) committed electronically using a computer.

DISSEISE To deprive of seisin (possession of land or other property).

FORENSICS The application of scientific knowledge to legal problems; the scientific analysis of physical evidence (such as evidence from a crime scene).

GENDARMERIE A body of soldiers especially in France serving as an armed police force for the maintenance of public order.

PREEMPTIVE Done to stop an unwanted act by another group, country, etc., from happening.

PREFECTURE Any one of the areas into which some countries (such as Japan and France) are divided for local government.

PROSECUTION The side of a legal case that argues that a person who is accused of a crime is guilty.

REPRISAL An act of retaliation.

TOTALITARIAN Of or relating to a political system in which the government has complete control over the people.

FOR MORE INFORMATION

Canadian Police College (CPC)
PO Box 8900
Ottawa, ON K1G 3J2
Canada
(613) 993-9501
Website: https://www.cpc.gc.ca/en

The CPC offers training and career development to law-enforcement officers throughout Canada, including specialized and advanced courses and workshops in investigative methods and forensics.

City of London Police Museum
Wood Street Police Station
37 Wood Street
London EC2P 2NQ
United Kingdom
Website: https://www.cityoflondon.police.uk/about-us/history/museum

This museum offers exhibits concerning the history of Britain's police service, the influence of social changes on police work, and modern policing techniques.

Federal Bureau of Investigation (FBI)
FBI Headquarters
935 Pennsylvania Avenue NW
Washington, DC 20535-0001
(202) 324-3000

Website: https://www.fbi.gov

The FBI investigates numerous crimes and national security concerns, including those involving terrorism, counterintelligence, cybercrimes, weapons of mass destruction, public corruption, civil rights, organized crime, white-collar crime, violent crime, and major thefts.

Interpol
General Secretariat
200, quai Charles de Gaulle
69006 Lyon
France
Website: http://www.interpol.int

The largest international police organization, Interpol allows police around the world to work together in combating crime and terrorism by providing tools, services, data, and secure communications channels.

Los Angeles Police Museum (LAPM)
6045 York Boulevard
Los Angeles, CA 90042
(323) 344-9445
Website: http://www.laphs.org

This museum's collection includes exhibits about famous officers and commissioners of the Los Angeles Police Department (LAPD) and police equipment and weapons used throughout the city's history.

Royal Canadian Mounted Police (RCMP)
Headquarters Building
73 Leikin Drive
Ottawa, ON K1A 0R2
Canada
(613) 993-7267
Website: http://www.rcmp-grc.gc.ca

The RCMP is Canada's federal police force. It also acts as the provincial and criminal police force in all territories except Ontario and Quebec.

US Department of Homeland Security
Website: http://www.dhs.gov

The Department of Homeland Security works to protect the United States and its inhabitants from various threats. Its mission includes securing and managing the nation's borders and administering immigration laws, preventing terrorism and enhancing security, safeguarding against cyberattacks, and responding to natural disasters or other large-scale emergencies. See https://www.dhs.gov/direct-contact-information to find the specific contact information for the department's various divisions.

WEBSITES

Because of the changing nature of internet links, Rosen Publishing has developed an online list of websites related to the subject of this book. This site is updated regularly. Please use this link to access the list:

http://www.rosenlinks.com/BLAW/case

FOR FURTHER READING

Albrecht, James F., Martha C. Dow, Darryl Plecas, and Dilip K. Das, eds. *Policing Major Events: Perspectives from Around the World*. Boca Raton, FL: CRC Press, 2015.

Anderson, Malcolm. *In Thrall to Political Change: Police and Gendarmerie in France*. New York, NY: Oxford University Press, 2011.

Bowman, Chris. *Police Officer* (Dangerous Jobs). Minneapolis, MN: Bellwether Media, 2015.

Britz, Marjie T. *Computer Forensics and Cyber Crime: An Introduction.* 3d ed. Boston, MA: Pearson, 2013.

Capsambelis, Chris. *Policing in Rural America: A Handbook for the Rural Law Enforcement Officer.* Durham, NC: Carolina Academic Press, 2009.

Collard, Sneed B. *The CIA and FBI: Top Secret.* Vero Beach, FL: Rourke Educational Media, 2014.

Dempsey, John S., and Linda S. Forst. *Police*. Clifton Park, NY: Delmar Cengage Learning, 2013.

Doak, Robin S. *National Intelligence* (Cornerstones of Freedom). New York, NY: Children's Press, 2013.

Espejo, Roman. *Community Policing* (Opposing Viewpoints). Farmington Hills, MI: Greenhaven Press, 2014.

Gerdes, Louise I., ed. *The 1992 Los Angeles Riots* (Perspectives on Modern World History). Farmington Hills, MI: Greenhaven Press, 2014.

Greve, Tom. *Police: Protect and Serve*. Vero Beach, FL: Rourke Educational Media, 2015.

Grinapol, Corinne. *Careers on Antiterrorism & Counterterrorism Task Forces* (Extreme Law Enforcement). New York, NY: Rosen Publishing, 2014.

Merino, Noël. *Civil Liberties* (Opposing Viewpoints). Farmington Hills, MI: Greenhaven Press, 2013.

Mullenbach, Cheryl. *Women in Blue: 16 Brave Officers, Forensics Experts, Police Chiefs, and More* (Women of Action). Chicago, IL: Chicago Review Press, 2016.

Philpott, Don. *Understanding the Department of Homeland Security*. Lanham, MD: Bernan Press, 2015.

Reisig, Michael Dean, and Robert J. Kane, eds. *The Oxford Handbook of Police and Policing*. New York, NY: Oxford University Press, 2014.

Roberg, Roy R. *Police & Society*. 6th ed. New York, NY: Oxford University Press, 2015.

Suen, Anastasia. *Careers with SWAT Teams* (Extreme Law Enforcement). New York, NY: Rosen Publishing, 2014.

Thompson, Tamara. *Domestic Surveillance*. Farmington Hills, MI: Greenhaven Press, 2015.

Vander Hook, Sue. *Miranda v. Arizona: An Individual's Rights When Under Arrest*. Minneapolis, MN: ABDO Publishing, 2013.

INDEX